Giggles

Jason King

PublishAmerica
Baltimore

First printing

ISBN: 1-4137-5659-X
PUBLISHED BY PUBLISHAMERICA, LLLP
www.publishamerica.com
Baltimore

Printed in the United States of America

Table of Contents

Action Movies

Action movies pack-a-punch!
I like to watch them while I munch

Kicks and spins!
Blown-up cars!

Lots of noise!
Movie stars...

Action movies pack-a-punch!
Plug one in
Have some fun

Apple

Give me the red one
Crunchy and sweet

Quenching my thirst
Plenty of meat

It's juicy I say
Why don't you eat?

There's one over there
Look at that tree

I feel better already
The cost was free

Maybe tomorrow
I'll try the green

Baby

One baby, two baby
Three baby, four
Out pokes her belly
She's having one more

One baby crawls
One baby leaps
One baby bawls
One baby sleeps

Precious little babies
Waiting for a bath
Waiting for some milk
Waiting for a nap

Out pokes her belly
She's having one more
It's time for a party
The baby is born

Baseball

We dip
We dive

We swing our bats

Throwing the ball
Tipping our hats

We love to steal
We love to slide

We love this game
The dream's alive

Basketball

Shoot a hoop
Make it fast

Pass the ball
Block the pass

Basketball...
The tall man's sport

Not for me
I play it short

Off the three
To the side

From the foul
Watch me drive

Billy's Snail

Chilly Billy
Found a snilly
Snail at grandpa's farm

Chilly Billy
Named him Willy
After thinking hard

He caught some more
He brought a sack
He filled it to the top

Snails for fish
Snails for glue
Snails for soda pop

Chilly Billy made his plans
And carefully pursued

Catching snails was not enough
So Billy reproduced

Bird

Hello up there
How are you doing?

You make too much noise
Stop quacking and cooing

I heard you already
Enough is enough

You're driving me crazy
And waking me up

I'll count to three
I'll count to ten

Hello up there
I hear you again

Birthday

It's my birthday
I want a party
Lots of gifts
I can hardly

Wait to make
A birthday wish
All those candles
Waiting lit

Food and cake
Fun for all
Ice cream too
A birthday song

Give me more
I just can't wait

Have some pie
In your face!

Blackbeard

Come aboard, step aside
The captain is here
The treasure we'll find

I smell it, it's near
There's no time for sleep
Bring me my map
And bring me the key

There's treasure out there
I'm certain of that
So bring out the brew
And bring me my hat

We're pirates at sea
So let's make a toast
Blackbeard is here
Who loves you the most!

Bounce

Bounce that ball
Loud and high

Throw it up
One more time

Have some fun
Kick it clear

Roll it
Toss it
Pass it here!

Breakfast

Extra meat
Lots of cheese
Lots of sauce
Make it sweet

Onions
Pickles
Tomatoes
Lettuce

Count me in
It's time for breakfast!

Broke

My motor is broke
Look at it smoke
I need a mechanic to find

The pieces that fit
That part that won't quit
Making that terrible noise

I need someone skilled
In engine rebuild
Someone to show me the way

My hood is up
My car is stuck
Soon I'll be towed away

Bugs

Little bugs stick to lights
Like bubblegum sticks to shoes

They bounce around
And catch a tan
Their eyes turn green and blue

Their feet get hot
Their brains on fire
Why don't they get a clue?

Little bugs stick to lights
Like bubblegum sticks to shoes

Car

My car is fast
My car is slow

Depending on
Which speed I go

I like to drive
I like to pass

I'm low on fuel
I need some gas

Chuck the Bucking Horse

Watch out for Chuck
He likes to Buck
He's Chuck the Bucking Horse

He doesn't think twice
So take my advice
He'll make your butt real sore

Just move to the side
And let him get by
He thinks kicking people is fun

And if that's not enough,
Watch him rear up
He'll knock you out with a punch

Watch out for Chuck
He likes to Buck
He's Chuck the Bucking Horse

Circus

Whistles and whips
Elephant tricks

Walking the rope
Acrobats fly

Clowns and stunts
Music and fun

The stilted man
How long can he stand!

It's circus time
It's all in a tent

Grab your seat
Bring a friend

Clock

Tick Tock goes the clock
Round and round go the hands

It's time to go
It's time to stay
It's time to wake the old man

We'll have some fun
We'll run away
We'll race the clock to the end

And when they say we're out of time
We'll race the clock again

Coffee

Hot coffee
Cold coffee
Tasting the taste

Bring me some cream
And sugar to chase

I'll have a tall Mocha
Or sweet Caramel
A creamy French Vanilla
A tasty new spell

A little whipped cream
A spark of caffeine
A jump in the morning
A second wind in the night

I'll take it black
But cream is preferred
A sip is never enough
I'll take all you can serve

Count

One, two
Tell the truth

Three, four
Hit the floor

Five, six
Make it quick

Seven, eight
Don't be late

Nine, ten
Tell me when

Eleven, twelve
Ring the bell

Thirteen, fourteen
Don't be boring

One, two
Tell the truth

Cowboy

Cowboy in the saddle,
Ready for battle

Leather in glove,
Gripping from above

Out through the gate,
The cowboy and his fate

Spurs digging in,
Reaching for the wind

The cowboy and the bronc
The eight-second flight

A cowboy takes a chance...
And always gets his ride

Crow

The crow at the top,
Quite simply I thought,
Would silence himself in the rain

Instead he kept on,
Until he was gone,
Forever withholding his name

His visit was short,
And briefly the sort,
That ends with him flying away

And though he was gone,
His chanting kept on,
Shouting from miles away

Crown

Kings and queens
Rule the scene
Heads begin to bow

The prince must wait
To know his fate
Perhaps he'll win the crowd

Knights will play
A fine display
Competing in the joust

The princess sleeps
And dreams of sheep,
Counting them aloud

Departure

What can I say...
Today is the day
We all must go
We cannot stay
We all must leave
And right away
No time to think
Today is the day

Disco

Take me to the disco
So I can dance and sing

So I can raise my hands
And hear the crowd scream

Take me to the disco
Where I can have some fun

And listen to the music
That really turns me on

I like to feel good
And have a good time

Take me to the disco
Where I can make you mine

Dog

I had a dog
That wouldn't bark

I gave a pat
It made him start

He barked all night
He barked all day

I gave him a bone
He raised his leg

Drink

Drink it up
Drink it down

Drink it all
Go to town

You'll love this flavor
You'll love the taste

Have some more
Drink away!

Fabrication

Machines are working
Gears are turning
Soon the parts will find...

Cuts and bends,
Sanded ends,
Changes in design

Holes are punched
Corners munched
Steady as a line

Machines are working
Gears are turning
Standard sets the time

Fireman

Crashing through the door,
He sweeps you off the floor

Calling in the team
Fire turns to steam

Ashes burn and smoke
Survival matters most

Up and down the ladder
In and out the door

In saving-people-matters
No one's keeping score

Fisherman

Into the water
He threw the chum

He waited with patience
The fish would soon come

The sun on his skin
The wind in his face

A boil at last
He'd waited all day

Food

Popcorn and chicken
Meat on the plate
Feed me some beans
A big juicy steak!

Pork sounds delicious
I'll give you a clue
Corn on the cob!
Potatoes and stew!

Cheesecake and pie
Ice cream and sweets
Lots of whipped cream
A shake is a treat

Give me the works
Cookies and all
Nothing too big
Nothing too small

Something to drink
Tasty and new
I'm under a spell!
Give me some food!

Gold

A nugget for me
A nugget for you

We'll search for gold
We'll pan the blue

This river's alive!
And full of wealth

We've got to look hard
And never tell

It's all for us
We're going to be rich!

Unload the mules
It's time to dig!

Hair

I wonder from under which way I
   should go
My hair is too long
There's no way to know

It covers my eyes
It covers my nose
It's down to my knees
It's touching my toes

I'd get a haircut, if I could afford
I'd use my old scissors
They're jammed in the drawer

I'd buzz it all off
The clipper is dead
I'd shave it away
But not with this set

I wonder from under which way I
   should go
My hair is too long
There's no way to know

Halloween

It's Halloween!
The scariest time
Have a treat
Close your eyes

Watch out for ghosts
Watch out for witches
The mummy's alive
The scarecrow twitches

And watch out for me
The scariest of them all
Your tiny little friend
Crawling on the wall

It's time for Halloween!
It's time for a fright
Open your eyes
It all starts tonight

Ice Cream

This ice cream is cold
It's colder than snow
I'm losing my mind in a swirl

It's colder than ice
I need some advice
There must be a crack in my bell!

The rush is on
When will it be gone?
The freezer is on in my head!

When will it be out?
How loud must I shout?
Give me some coffee instead!

Journey

Take it away,
To find it again

Nothing is lost
Unless you give in

Tough is a challenge
Fun is a game

Reaching a balance
Requires a change

To find your way back,
Think in reverse

Continue ahead,
By shifting to first

Jumping Jack

Jumping Jack
Hit the sack
He felt so tired and sleepy

Soon I'll be home
And no one will know
The secret that I have been keeping

For now I will dream
Of wonderful things
Nothing is better than sleeping

Jumping Jack
Hit the sack
He felt so tired and sleepy

Kitchen

The kitchen is clean,
And now I can see,
Everything sparkling bright

Before I came here
Nothing was clear
Now it's a beautiful sight

Washing the dishes
Takes some time
Scrubbing the counter
Cleans the grime

Washing the stove...
Stacking the plates
Wiping the cups
Storing the grapes

Everything counts
Not one little mess
My kitchen is clean
But look at my dress

Light

That light is too bright
Try turning it down

I'm losing my sight
You're turning me brown

I see you just fine
You're wearing a gown

That light is too bright
Try turning it down

Lighthouse

Up the stairs
To the light
All is well
For vessel sight

Down the stairs
Of this old house
The light is bright
The lost are found

Lunch

Shake the salt
Shake the pepper
Cook the food
How's the weather?

Couldn't be better
A perfect day
What's for lunch?
Fish you say!

What kind of fish?
It must be trout
You might be right
Try it out!

Sure enough
Trout it is!
Delicious too
But what is this?

It's just a bone
Throw it out!
And have a drink
It's on the house!

Men at Work

Clinking and clanking,
The men are at work

Chopping and chipping,
Preparing for girth

Adjusting the frame
Constructing the chassis

Bending, dividing,
Attaching and scrapping

The men are at work,
Welding away

Sparks in the air,
Attempting to change

It's time for a torch
It's time for a saw

Pass me that wrench
Watch for my draw

Mess

The crumbs are out!
You made a mess!
So don't deny...
You must confess!

It's not the first,
It's not the last
Mess you've made,
In the past

You made a mess
So don't deny
You must confess!
So holler I

Muscle

Pump me up
Add another weight

Another 10 pounds
Another 58

Make my body grow
Make my muscles ache

Take me to the gym
Help me get in shape

One day I'll be big
One day I'll be strong...

Posing on a stage,
Flexing to a song

The crowd will scream and shout
The judges will stare

Take me to the gym,
So I can prepare

Mystery Dog

He likes to howl
And bark at the moon
My schemish friend
Who wears no shoe

His coat is thick
His hair is long
He's like a wolf
He's very calm

And though I feed him
Day and night
He's always hungry
For a bite

He likes to howl
And bark at the moon
My schemish friend
Who wears no shoe

Painter

I painted the wall
I painted my hand
I painted the clock
I painted the fan

I painted all day
I painted all night
When she entered the room
I painted her white

I painted the mirror
I painted the floor
I painted the light
I painted the door

I painted with brush
I painted with spray
Painting is fun
I painted all day

Peeping Tom

The peeping Tom
Took too long
And fell from
A very high branch

He must have forgot
To hide his binocs
The neighbors were
Playing with them

Some people laughed
Some people frowned
Why are you spying on us?

The peeping Tom
Ran along
And never came back again

Rocks

The rocks are aligned,
Together assigned...
The shape and the size of a flock

Front is to back
Back is to front,
Together upholding a block

A linear course,
A bumpier line,
A way of controlling the road

Everyone sees
The work that's been done...
And everyone follows it home

Runaway Rocket

Up and away!
Into the sky
Runaway rocket
Into the night

Watching it go
Far and away
Watching it now
Never too late

The runaway rocket
Climbs and explodes
Finding a path
Taking the show

Up and away!
Into the sky
Runaway rocket
Into the night

Safari

Lions and tigers
Sheep and goat

Birds and bears
Wolves and toad

I'm on a safari
I live on a boat

I'm watching a snake
He's crossing the road

Sail

We sailed the sea
We sailed the sky
Our quest to live
The wind alive

A storm we hit
And by surprise
And though it struck,
We stayed our eye

We must have climbed
A thousand walls...
Of twisted sea
And waterfall

We focused ahead...
The sailor's goal...
Our destiny,
To free the soul

Sam the Ghost

Ooky spooky Sam the Ghost
Scares us all
Like pop-up toast

He waits until it's nice and dark
And tries to shock your beating heart

It's dark in here
Turn on the light

You're scaring me
And that's a fright

The ooky spooky ghost will wait
He'll hide inside until it's late

And when you sleep he'll creep up close
And scream that he's a crazy ghost!

He's not your friend
So watch for Boo!
Ooky spooky Sam wants you

Shapes

Geometric prisms...
Circles, squares, and shapes

Running through my mind,
Lines without a place

Ninety-nine degrees...
Patterns on the ground

Floating in the air...
Patterns all around

Sheik

At last,
A camel,
Something to ride

To walk through this desert
I'd never survive

Who would have thought...
A sheik out of me

This one lonely rebel
Was happy and free

Where is my tribe?
They all ran away...

They left me to suffer
The heat of the day

Shells

Shells, shells
Lots of shells

Different sizes
Here to sell

Buy one now
Get one free

Buy a few
Two or three

Shells, shells
Lots of shells

Make a chime
Make a bell

Buy a few
Two or three

Lots of shells
From the sea

Shoe

Darn this shoe!
It just won't fit

I've stretched
I've pulled
I've tugged
I've bit!

I've jerked
I've gnawed
I've jumped
I've kicked

Darn this shoe!
It just won't fit

Show

Let's go
Why not?
It's time
Why stop?

The sign says enter
The show will begin
Our seats are waiting
I'm heading in

What's that you say?
There's danger inside
What kind of danger?
Where and why?

It couldn't be much
I'm going anyway
Thanks for the warning
I'll see you another day

Soldier

Courage and confidence,
Heart and pride

Play it smart...
To stay alive

I'm ready to serve,
Raise my flag

Call my name,
Toss my hat

Surprise

Today's your birthday!
On your feet
Out of bed
No more sleep

Have some pie
Eat some cake
Try a chocolate
Bellyache

Time to laugh
Time to sing
Make a wish
Count to three

Today's your birthday!
On your feet
Out of bed
No more sleep

Thief

Stop that thief!
The one with the sack
He took it from me
And I want it back

He stole it away
Before I could see
His devious plan
To steal it from me

Start chasing him down!
Start calling him names!
Try throwing a rock!
Or tripping his leg!

He took it from me
And I want it back
Stop that thief!
The one with the sack

Toad

The toad in the road
Went splishety-splash
In puddles that lay ahead

No car did he trust
Not even the bus
That carefully drove
Past his head

On his way home
The toad was alone
But soon he would be
With his friends

Then they would play
In puddles all day
Splashing and making
A mess

Toy

Speed up
Slow down

Make it fly
Hit the ground

I love this toy
It never breaks

I want another
Just in case

Crash, Bash!
Bang, Boom!
Smash, Squash!
Stretch, Zoom!

I love this toy
It never breaks
I want another
Just in case

Train

Clear the track!
The train is coming

Move away!
It stops for nothing

Watch it steam
Hear it roar

Step inside
All aboard

Right on time
As usual

My ticket's here
My bags are full

Clear the track!
It stops for nothing

All aboard!
The train is coming

Trashman

Here's to the man
Who throws a can,
And drives a truck
That crushes stuff

Here's to the man
Who turns the wheel,
To aim the forks
That meet the steel

That bring it up
And empty out,
All the junk
That we throw out...

The guy that fights
That terrible stench...
And dumps it out,
Here's to him

Here's to the man
Who throws a can
Thanks to him,
The trashman

Victory

Over the hill
Under the sun

Feeling alive...
The beat of the drum

We pounded,
We sang,
We danced,
We spun,

Feeling alive...
The beat of the drum

Zoo

Take me to the zoo
So I can see what's new

The animals at play
The signs to show the way

Take me to the zoo
Where tired monkeys snooze

Giraffes stand tall
Gorillas crawl
Baby tigers chew

Take me when I'm blue
So I can pick and choose

My favorite friend
To see again
Take me to the zoo

Printed in the United Kingdom
by Lightning Source UK Ltd.
106560UKS00001B/184